In Collaboration with Nike

REBEL GiRLS

Kick it

World Champions Take the Pitch—and You Can Too

This is a work of creative nonfiction. It is a collection of heartwarming and thought-provoking stories inspired by the life and adventures of 28 amazing athletes. It is not an encyclopedic account of the events and accomplishments of their lives.

www.rebelgirls.com

Art director: Giulia Flamini
Cover designer: Kristen Brittain
Graphics designer: Georgia Rucker
Editor: Jess Harriton
Text by: Alexis Stratton, Frances Thomas, Jess Harriton, and Tatyana White-Jenkins

ISBN: 979-8-88964-082-0

CONTENTS

Dear Rebels,

For as long as I can remember, I have loved sport. I love sport not just for the way it makes me feel physically and mentally, but also for everything it has given to me, my life, my family, and so many people across the world. Sport brings so much joy, whether one is playing or watching. Sport has a unique way of uniting people that I find incredible.

My parents moved from Ghana to the United Kingdom in the late '60s, and football helped them find friends and navigate a new country. For me, from the moment I could walk, I was running, then jumping. I was always moving! I simply couldn't live without the thrill and energy that sport gave me. Playing sports gave me physical skills, and taught me life skills that I still use everyday both at home and at work.

I particularly enjoyed team sports like football, netball, and field hockey. Being part of a team is a great way to connect with a supportive group. Team sports teach us to value one another's unique roles and differences, and to work together to be the best you can be. You have a common language and common goal. You learn to take a sense of 'we' with you wherever you go in life. Sport helped me discover myself and define the personal values that I hold today.

My kids love football. We come from a football family; my father was (and still is for his age) an incredible footballer. And my mother and my husband are both huge football fans. We really do live and breathe the sport. We recently moved to the USA, and football has helped our children make friends and find joy incredibly quickly. It is the common language they can speak wherever they are. When I look to my son and my daughter, I see that sport is giving them the same things it gave me. I'm passionate about them moving their bodies, and I feel very fortunate I am able to give them those opportunities to move in any way they can or want.

My job is actually my passion; how lucky am I? I know that not every child has the opportunity to have sport in their lives. Girls especially still face barriers that make it hard for them to be seen and heard in sport. I'm in a position now to contribute to making a change. And thankfully things are changing for the better, with women's football leading the charge. Here at Nike, we can help change happen faster. We are committed to helping create a world where every child can experience the power of play and sport. We know that sport unites people and can move the world forward.

The momentum behind women's football is phenomenal and we are thrilled to be part of it. We work with athletes, teams, and federations to provide more access for girls to play sport. We know that sport can help girls like you navigate some of those trickier moments of growing up. It builds inner confidence and provides so much joy—who doesn't want that?

Nike worked on the biggest football tournament in 2019, and we saw firsthand the incredible impact it had on women's football. We can only imagine what is about to happen in this year's world championship. These inspirational athletes and their teams are leading the way. They are showing us what football can be for the next generation to come.

So the stage is set for yet another transformational tournament. Millions of people will be watching, and the joy and passion will be palpable. Yet again a new generation of athletes will be inspired to play. I hope you will be one of them.

STEPHANIE ANKRAH
Vice President, Global Brand Management Kids, Nike Inc.

Ada was at the top of her game when her career screeched to a halt.

Ada had started her professional football career at 15 years old. She became a top scorer, and each time she scored, she threw her arms out and ran to her teammates like she was flying, a huge smile on her face. As the years went by, Ada's career rose like a rocket.

Then one day, during training, something popped in Ada's leg. Suddenly, she couldn't walk, and the pain was unbearable. When she was finally able to train again, she found out she had a stress fracture in her leg too!

Ada didn't play football for almost two years. Her body needed time to heal, but Ada struggled to be patient. *Will I ever get to play again?* she thought.

Eventually, Ada's legs were strong enough to run, and as she trained, she felt like a kid falling in love with football for the first time.

Ada believes that her renewed passion for her sport just might help her break even more records. She can't wait to take the pitch at her fourth world championship.

FUN FACT

Ada's older sister, Andrine, is also a professional footballer. The two have played together for Norway's national team—and against each other in club matches across Europe.

In 2018, Ada won France's first-ever Ballon d'Or Féminin, a prize for the best woman footballer.

'MY BIGGEST AMBITION IS TO MAXIMISE THE POTENTIAL IN ME.'
—Ada Hegerberg

AITANA BONMATÍ

Midfielder

Spain • Born 18 January 1998

Aitana always felt like she was born to play football. But piano, guitar, English—those were the things that Aitana's parents wanted her to learn. So, Aitana plunked away at keys and strummed clumsily at strings—all while staring out the window, imagining herself running down a football pitch with the wind in her hair.

When Aitana kicked a football, every fibre in her cried out, *I am meant for this!*

But no matter how good she was, kids picked on her. They said girls shouldn't play football.

Am I doing something wrong? she wondered.

But Aitana listened to the voice inside her that told her to follow her dream. Eventually, Aitana's parents signed her up for a team. By 13, she was recruited for Barcelona's youth academy. A few years later, she went pro.

Today, Aitana is one of Spain's star players. She still has a guitar and loves reading, but when she's on the pitch, it's clear: Aitana and football are meant for each other.

FUN FACT

Aitana listens to upbeat songs to pump her up before a big match. Some of her favourites are classic jams like 'Eye of the Tiger' by Survivor and 'It's My Life' by Bonjovi.

Before matches, Aitana likes to get in the zone by doing visualizations and breathing exercises. These help calm her body and clear her mind. Here's a simple breathing exercise to try before a game to help you focus too:

- Find a comfortable place to sit. You can sit either cross-legged or with your feet on the floor.

- Place one hand on your belly and one hand on your chest. Take a moment to notice how you're feeling today.

- Take a deep breath in through your nose for several seconds. Feel the air fill your lungs and your belly expand.

- Then, slowly blow the air out through your mouth like you're blowing out birthday candles.

- Repeat these steps several times. Check in with yourself when you're done—how are you feeling now?

'TO SUCCEED, IT'S NEVER ENOUGH TO HAVE THE TALENT. YOU NEED . . . HUNGER TO BECOME THE BEST AND NEVER STOP GROWING.'
—Aitana Bonmati

ALEX MORGAN

Forward

United States • Born 2 July 1989

Growing up, Alex Morgan dreamed of becoming a professional athlete. She played *everything*. Some days, her parents drove her from softball practice to football practice and then to a basketball game. In high school, though, football became Alex's favorite.

Alex fought through injuries and setbacks to make her way to the top—becoming a pro player and, eventually, a member of the US National Women's Team.

There she was, 21 years old, in the historic city of Padua, Italy, at a world championship qualifying tournament. The United States needed to win their match against Italy to secure their spot.

When Alex took to the pitch in overtime, the score was 0-0. Her instructions were clear: go for the goal. Alex received a pass from her teammate. Darting past defenders, she approached the goal and—*BAM*! Her powerful kick launched the ball into the net just past the goalie. Alex jumped into the arms of her teammates. She'd just secured her team's place on the biggest stage of all.

FUN FACT

Alex Morgan is also an author. Her 12-book young readers series The Kicks explores themes of football, fun, friendship—and learning to believe in yourself. It was even made into a TV series.

One of Alex's favourite pregame meals is banana pancakes. Maybe they'll be your favourite too!

Ingredients

- 125 g (1 cup) all-purpose flour
- 15 g (1 tbsp) baking powder
- ½ teaspoon cinnamon
- ¼ teaspoon salt
- 115 g (¾ cup) mashed ripe banana
- 1 large egg
- 180 ml (¾ cup) milk

Instructions

In a medium bowl, whisk together flour, baking powder, cinnamon, and salt.

In larger bowl, beat the banana and egg together until blended. Add the milk and whisk until combined. Next, add the dry ingredients and whisk until combined.

Heat a large pan over medium heat. Spray with nonstick cooking spray.

Using a ⅓-cup measuring cup, pour 3 or 4 circles of batter into the pan. Cook 2 to 3 minutes or until the pancakes are puffed on top and golden brown on the bottom. Then flip and cook on the other side 1 to 2 minutes more.

'ALWAYS WORK HARD, NEVER GIVE UP, AND FIGHT UNTIL THE END, BECAUSE IT'S NEVER REALLY OVER UNTIL THE WHISTLE BLOWS.'
—Alex Morgan

ASISAT OSHOALA

Every day after school, Asisat played football in the streets of her hometown of Lagos in Nigeria. She would return home with bruises and skinned knees, but to her, there was nothing better. Asisat's parents weren't supportive of her spending so much time on football, though. For a long time, Asisat didn't consider playing football professionally.

One day, Asisat was playing in a local tournament. As usual, she brought her all to the pitch: sprinting, passing, and scoring. A coach asked her if she would join their team. Asisat felt a pang in her heart. She knew her parents wouldn't approve. She had to say no.

Asisat continued to play on the side while studying at university. It wasn't until her stunning performance in the U-20 women's world championship that she realised she was good enough to be a professional footballer. She was the highest goal scorer in the tournament! That night, she won the Golden Ball and Golden Boot trophies. Asisat never gave up and ultimately followed her heart where it told her to go.

DID YOU KNOW?

In some tied matches, players have to participate in a shoot-out to determine the winner. In a shoot-out, each team has a number of chances to try and kick the ball into the other team's goal, with only their goalkeeper defending it. The team with the most goals is deemed the winner.

Asisat is the first African woman to win the Pichichi Trophy, which is given to the top scorer in the Spanish league.

'ONE THING I KNOW IS THAT YOU CAN FIGHT OVER YOUR FEAR. YOU CAN CHANGE THE WHOLE WORLD WITH YOUR COURAGE.'
—Asisat Oshoala

BARBARA BONANSEA

Forward and Midfielder

Italy • Born 13 June 1991

Growing up, Barbara and her brother often played football in the courtyard of their house, kicking the ball against the building's walls. When her family watched football on TV, Barbara cheered for Cristiano Ronaldo and dreamed of pulling off his signature knuckleball free kick—a strike that sends the ball wobbling unpredictably through the air at a high speed.

But Barbara didn't play on a team. Instead, she tagged along with her brother when he practised with his teammates at their local club. Secretly, she wished she could join them.

Then, one day, the coach walked over to where Barbara was sitting. *Will you come play with us?* he asked.

Those six little words made Barbara's heart soar. She raced onto the pitch.

Over time, Barbara became a speedy midfielder, making crucial assists and epic long-range goals. With a flick of her foot, she could fake out opponents, dribbling away before they even realised she'd stolen the ball! And today, she wows the world with her knuckleball free kick as thousands of fans cheer her on.

> 'I WANT TO BE AN EXAMPLE FOR YOUNG GIRLS BECAUSE, WHEN I MEET THEM, I SEE MYSELF IN THEIR EYES, WHICH ARE FULL OF DREAMS AND ASPIRATIONS.'
>
> —Barbara Bonansea

The knuckleball free kick is tricky, but with practise you can master it, just like Barbara!

* **Set Yourself Up:** Start four to six steps away from the ball and one or two steps to the left or right, depending on the foot you'll be kicking with.

* **Approach:** Run toward the ball. When you're ready to kick, plant your non-kicking foot beside the ball. Make sure your toes point in the direction you want the ball to go.

* **Strike:** Kick the ball just below its centre. The contact point of your foot should be between your instep and ankle joint. Keep your ankle locked firmly.

* **Stop Your Follow-Through:** As soon as you make contact, stop your kicking leg from following through. Some players recommend hopping after the strike and planting your foot where the ball was.

FUN FACT

Barbara has a degree in business economics.

DRILL BREAK: SOCKS OFF

Roll up a pair of socks—clean or smelly—and grab an empty laundry basket, bin, or bag.

EASY

- Place the basket four steps away.
- Start by holding the sock ball in your hand.
- Drop the ball and kick it towards the basket. Give yourself **five points** for each one you get **in** the basket.
- Give yourself **one point** each time you **hit** the basket. How many points can you get in 10 attempts?
- Can you beat your best score?

- When you're ready, try this with your other (nondominant) foot.
- If you get one in the basket, give yourself **10 points**.
- If you hit the basket, give yourself **five points**.
- Can you beat your best score? How did you do it?

WITH FRIENDS AND FAMILY

- When you're ready, challenge a friend or family member to the same game.
- Take turns until you have each made 10 attempts. Who got the higher score? How did they do it?
- What can you learn from your partner's attempts? Tell your partner two things you think they did well during their turn.

YOU CAN ALSO THROW THE SOCKS IF YOU WANT TO!

KHADIJA 'BUNNY' SHAW

Forward

Jamaica • Born 31 January 1997

Khadija always knew there was something special about football. The speed of the game, the exciting tricks, and the passion she saw from players and fans made her eyes grow wide. One day, instead of just watching the boys in her community play in the street, she decided to jump right in!

Sometimes Khadija felt like she wasn't good enough to compete with the boys. But she kept practising. Soon, Khadija gained more confidence. She learned that not only was football special—she was too. Khadija thought to herself, *I could be the one to change football in Jamaica.*

She was right. Khadija's breakout performance was in a match that would determine if Jamaica was going to the 2019 world championship. She used her powerful, precise footwork to score the incredible goals that helped her team secure the win. It was Jamaica's first time ever qualifying for the world championship! Khadija was so proud of this historic accomplishment.

DID YOU KNOW?

Reggae singer Bob Marley's daughter, Cedella Marley, is credited with resurrecting women's football in Jamaica! When the Jamaica's women's football team, known as the Reggae Girlz, was about to be dissolved due to lack of funding, Cedella sponsored the team through the Bob Marley Foundation.

18

Khadija was nicknamed 'Bunny' by her brother Kentardo because of her love of carrots at an early age.

'WORK HARD AND STAY COMMITTED EVEN WHEN MISTAKES HAPPEN.'
—Khadija 'Bunny' Shaw

CHLOE KELLY

Forward

England • Born 15 January 1998

Chloe Kelly grew up in West London playing football with her five older brothers. They played on paved streets and in the city's 'cages'—fenced-in pitches where games became rough-and-tumble battles.

Chloe was usually the only girl, but she didn't mind. No matter where she went, she had a ball at her feet and was ready to play.

When Chloe got older, she moved north to play professionally for Manchester City. Scrappy and fierce, she seemed destined for success. But in 2021, Chloe suffered a serious leg injury that sent her to the sidelines.

Her fans worried she might be gone for good. But Chloe worked hard at rehab—and almost a year later, she was back playing for England's national team.

In the 2022 Women's Euro finals, England was tied 1–1 with Germany. In extra time, Chloe took a shot—and was blocked. When she got the ball again, she kicked as hard as she could. The ball soared through the air, past the keeper and into the net— GOAL!

Chloe's team swarmed the field. She had just helped them bring home England's first major trophy in women's football.

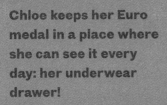

FUN FACT

Chloe keeps her Euro medal in a place where she can see it every day: her underwear drawer!

'I DON'T REALLY HAVE THOSE NERVES [AS I DID BEFORE] BECAUSE I'M THINKING: 'WHAT'S THE WORST THAT CAN HAPPEN?' I'VE BEEN THROUGH THE WORST. I HAVE TO ENJOY EVERY MOMENT, PLAYING WITH NO FEAR.'
—Chloe Kelly

CHRISTINE SINCLAIR

Forward

Canada • Born 12 June 1983

Christine's amazing journey in football started when she was just four years old. Since there wasn't a team for girls her age, she joined a boys' team, the Burnaby Bees, when she was six years old.

Playing with bigger kids made Christine feel a little uneasy, but it also made her a better player. She dreamed of being as good as her idols, Mia Hamm and Michelle Akers. And with her gifted goal-scoring touch, she was well on her way.

At just 16 years old, Christine had her breakout moment. She hopped on her first international flight, put on her shiny, new red-and-white uniform, and competed for the Canadian Women's National team in the 2000 Algarve Cup. She made a great first impression, using swift, powerful kicks to score three goals during the tournament. And during the cup, Christine found herself sharing an elevator with Mia Hamm and Michelle Akers! She was starstruck.

Now, having played the sport professionally for more than 20 years, Christine loves inspiring young girls to pursue football even if it's scary at first.

'APPRECIATE THE HARD WORK ON THE FIELD AND THE WORK YOU DO OFF OF IT TO ADVANCE THE GAME. IT'S ALL WORTH IT TO LEAVE FOOTBALL BETTER THAN YOU FOUND IT.'
—Christine Sinclair

YOUR TURN!

Want to practise like Christine? Try juggling! It's a great way to learn control over the football.

* First, practise the flick up. With the football on the ground, place your foot on top of it to roll it towards you. Then, while it's rolling, move your foot to the bottom of the ball to scoop it up into the air with the top of your foot.

* Catch the ball with the top of your foot or your knee.

* Kick the ball up and then catch it again with the top of your other foot or your other knee.

* Keep going and count how many times you can juggle the ball without losing control of it.

ESMEE BRUGTS

Forward

The Netherlands • Born 28 July 2003

As a child, Esmee Brugts tried lots of sports. More than anything, though, she loved kicking around a football with her classmates.

But there wasn't a girls' football team in her village. So when Esmee was six, she started running drills with the boys.

Esmee played on the boys' team until she was 16, when her fabulous footwork caught the eye of the Dutch Football Association. Soon, Esmee was plucked from her village team and moved into the highest level of women's football in the Netherlands.

Two years later, Esmee made her senior debut with her national team in a match against Brazil. She was the youngest player representing the Netherlands, but her fast feet and solid shots made her stand out.

One of Esmee's biggest contributions came at the end of a scoreless match against Iceland in September 2022. In the 93rd minute, Esmee sent a cross into the box. The ball sailed right past the defenders—and *thwacked* into the net!

Thanks to Esmee's incredible goal, the Netherlands won the match—and secured their spot in the world championship.

> 'FOOTBALL IS MY JOY.
> IT MAKES ME HAPPY.'
> —Esmee Brugts

A *cross* is when a player delivers the football from one side of the pitch to the box—the area in front of the goal. (Or in Esmee's case, in the goal!) There are many types of crosses, including chip crosses, inswinging crosses, outswinging crosses, and low crosses.

YOUR TURN!

Here are three tips for crossing a football:

* **Take It Slow:** Practise crossing with a stationary ball before trying with a rolling ball.

* **Dodge Defenders:** Defenders in the way? Beat them by kicking the ball past them before you cross.

* **Watch for Teammates:** Crossing is often used to set up a teammate's goal. So practise crossing to different parts of the box (not just the middle) so you can learn to set up your forwards to score big.

FRAN KIRBY

Forward

England • Born 29 June 1993

The day of Fran's first football practise, she refused to go. All of the players on the team were older than seven-year-old Fran, and she was nervous!

Fran's mum knew she just needed encouragement. She convinced her to try it out, and soon, Fran was hooked. In no time, Fran perfected her passes, traps, and goal shots. Her mum loved to see Fran play, and Fran loved to see her mum smiling from the stands.

But when Fran was 14, her mum passed away suddenly. Fran missed her so much that she quit football altogether.

A few years later, Fran's friend asked her to join an amateur league. Fran was still sad, but after a few friendly games, she was ready to pursue her dream of going pro.

Today, Fran is a valuable scorer for Chelsea Football Club and England's national team. Whether she's blasting the ball into the net or slipping it past the keeper, her shots are always impressive. Even though her mum isn't here, Fran knows she would be proud.

DID YOU KNOW?

It has been reported that crowds of 10,000 spectators would watch women play football in North London in the 1890s. During the First World War, the women's game really took off since many men were away fighting.

FUN FACT

When Fran first played football, she wasn't scoring goals—she was stopping them! Her first position was goalie.

'EVERY TIME I SCORE, I CELEBRATE LIKE THE KID I WAS PLAYING IN THE PARK.'
—Fran Kirby

DRILL BREAK: HOW MANY TOUCHES?

**Make a small circle on the ground or floor using cones, chalk, blocks—whatever you can find!
Then, grab a football.**

EASY

- Set a timer for 30 seconds.
- How many touches with your feet can you make within the 30-second timeframe without the ball leaving the circle?
- Can you beat your best score?

- Set a timer for 30 seconds.
- This time, try touching the ball with as many different parts of your feet as possible, like your toe, laces, sole, heel, and the inside and outside of your foot.
- How many touches can you make in the 30-second timeframe?
- For an extra challenge, set the timer again, and try to play without using the same part of your foot twice in a row.
- What is it you did well when you got your best score?

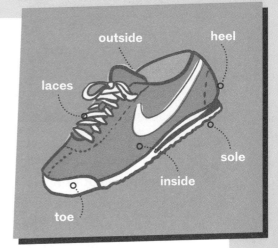

WITH FRIENDS AND FAMILY

- When you're ready, get a friend or family member to join you in the challenge.
- See how many touches you can get in 30 seconds, but this time take turns between touches.
- Think about how you can get the most touches as a team.

GIULIA GWINN

Midfielder

Germany • Born 2 July 1999

When Giulia injured her knee during a big match, she was devastated. It was going to take almost a year for her to be back playing with her team again.

In the hospital and during her first weeks in physical therapy, waves of sadness washed over her. But there was a silver lining: She had a recovery buddy. Her teammate Jovana was injured at the same time. Slowly, the two women became closer, sharing their small wins like walking normally, then running, then jumping.

Together, they went to their team's games and cheered from the sidelines. Every time Germany scored, the players on the pitch ran to Giulia and Jovana for a group hug.

Soon, the weeks were flying by, and finally, Giulia got the okay to play in the next match. She was thrilled.

The whole day felt magical. Giulia found herself relishing little things she had taken for granted before, like seeing her jersey waiting for her in the locker room.

Now, both Giulia and Jovana are back on the pitch and stronger than ever.

DID YOU KNOW?

In Giulia's debut world championship match in 2019, she scored a goal from inside the box, helping her team win 1–0 against China. She was the third teenager to score for Germany in women's world championship history—and she won the Young Player of the Tournament award.

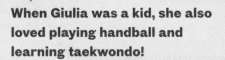

FUN FACT

When Giulia was a kid, she also loved playing handball and learning taekwondo!

'I REALISED THAT I WAS ABLE TO FIGHT BACK AND I HAVE MORE SELF-CONFIDENCE NOW.'
—Giulia Gwinn

GRACE GEYORO

Midfielder

France • Born 2 July 1997

When Grace Geyoro was eight years old, she stepped onto the football pitch in her hometown of Orleáns, France. Around her was a squad full of boys. Grace was the first—and only—girl on the team.

A lot of people thought it was strange for Grace to play football. Even her mom, Angelique, said the game wasn't suitable for girls. But Grace's brother convinced their mom that Grace was not only good—she was *great*.

Grace was so good that at 15, she started training at Paris Saint-Germain (PSG), a pro football club. And in 2017, at 19 years old, Grace became a professional footballer at PSG.

By 2022, Grace was a favourite on the French national team. And in their 2022 Euro match against Italy, she wowed the crowd by becoming the first player to score a hat trick in the first half of a women's Euro match!

After Grace's third goal, she formed her hands into a heart and pointed it toward her family's seats. Angelique—now Grace's biggest fan—cheered the loudest of them all.

FUN FACT

Before a big match, Grace gets in the zone by putting on her headphones and listening to Afrobeats. 'Ayo' by Simi and 'Free Mind' by Tems are examples of Afrobeats. Give them a listen and see if they pump you up to play too!

DID YOU KNOW?

A *hat trick* is when a single player scores three goals in a football match. The word *brace* is used when a player scores twice!

HAYLEY RASO

Midfielder

Australia • Born 5 September 1994

Hayley Raso grew up on Australia's Gold Coast. She was confident swimming and splashing in the ocean, but at school Hayley was shy.

One day, the local football team held tryouts. As Hayley learned to pass and dribble, something shifted inside her. It was just like at the beach. Her worries lifted, and she didn't feel shy anymore. Hayley made the team, and her nan gave her a beautiful ribbon to celebrate. *Wear this for strength*, said Nan, tying it in a bow around Hayley's ponytail. Since that day, Hayley's never played without it.

The ribbon has followed her all the way from the local football team to some of the biggest tournaments in the world. It kept her strong through the highest highs and the lowest lows—like when she broke her back in an accident on the pitch. Hayley wasn't sure she'd walk again, let alone play football. But after six months of intensive rehab, she laced up her boots. She scored a goal in her first game back!

This year, she can't wait to represent her country at the biggest football tournament on her home soil. Nan and the rest of her family will be cheering from the sidelines. No matter where you watch the games from, it'll be easy to spot her—just look for the bright ribbon.

> 'ENJOY YOURSELF! KEEP PRACTISING. DON'T LET ANYONE TELL YOU THAT YOU AREN'T GOOD ENOUGH.'
> —Hayley Raso

Hayley is a bit superstitious—before a game, she turns her socks inside out and always puts her left one on before her right one.

YOUR TURN!

When you're playing football or any sport, it's helpful to have your hair out of your face. But sporty hairstyles don't have to be boring—just ask Hayley! She wears a colourful ribbon in her hair every time she plays—and you can too. Pick a ribbon in your favourite colour, and ask a friend to tie it around your ponytail, braid, or bun before your next match or practise. Every time you run for the ball, you'll feel your special ribbon dancing in the wind behind you.

Once there was a girl who was torn between two sports. At 17, Jackie was a footballer and a judoka—someone who competes in judo, a form of martial arts from Japan.

Jackie made it onto her first professional football team when she was a teenager, and she kept competing in national judo tournaments. Once, though, Jackie had to tell her football coaches that she'd hurt her hip during a judo competition and couldn't play.

She knew she had to make a choice: It was one sport or the other.

Football was so exciting. The lights! The speed! The bond of a team! But she also felt drawn to the discipline of judo. Jackie thought and thought. She tried to picture her future in each sport. She relived the rush of slamming a ball straight past the goalkeeper and the glory of tossing her opponent onto the mat.

Finally, Jackie made her decision—and dashed out onto the pitch.

Now, when she and her teammates are in sync, passing and scoring and laughing, she knows she made the right choice. And she has never looked back.

FUN FACT

Jackie plays guitar and loves collecting vintage records by bands like Fleetwood Mac, Queen, and the Beatles.

'DEEP DOWN, I THINK I ALWAYS KNEW IT WAS GOING TO BE FOOTBALL.' —Jackie Groenen

DID YOU KNOW?

When Jackie was growing up, she was a huge Manchester United fan—and in 2019, she became the first non-British player to sign with Manchester United women's team.

JÉSSICA SILVA

Forward and Midfielder

Portugal • Born 11 December 1994

From the time Jéssica Silva started playing football, she dreamed of taking Portugal's women's team to the world championship.

Jéssica's father had been a professional footballer, and though he died when she was young, his passion remained in her. As Jéssica got older, her fancy footwork made her look like she was dancing down the pitch, and she became known for her speed, tricks, and nutmegs.

Jéssica made her senior debut for Portugal in 2011, but each time her team tried for the world championship, they lost. Finally, in 2022, Jéssica donned her red Portugal jersey for another big match against Iceland. This match was important because it was a step toward qualifying for the world championship.

But Jéssica's heart was heavy. That morning, she had gotten terrible news: Her grandmother had died. As she dashed across the field, though, she imagined her grandmother and father looking down on her, cheering for her still. She promised to play well for them.

With Jéssica's magical moves, Portugal beat Iceland 4–1 that day—and soon after, they finally secured their spot in their first-ever world championship.

FUN FACT

Along with football, Jéssica loves playing guitar, skateboarding, reading poetry, dancing, and hanging out with her family.

Nutmeg describes when a player passes a ball between a defender's legs. It was first used as slang in the 1800s to describe being deceived—and comes from the notorious practises of dishonest nutmeg merchants, who often tricked buyers by selling them wooden nutmeg seeds.

'IT'S NOT ALWAYS BEEN EASY FOR ME—I'VE HAD TO FACE A LOT OF OBSTACLES AND FIGHTS TO GET HERE— BUT THIS IS THE MOMENT I DREAMED OF.'
—Jéssica Silva

KADEISHA BUCHANAN

Defender

Canada • Born 5 November 1995

Kadeisha is a skilled defender on the pitch. She can shut down some of the best strikers in the world. Playing centre-back, Kadeisha is like a shadow, anticipating her opponents' every move and outthinking their every step. Then, she strikes, stealing the ball or blocking their plays.

But when Kadeisha was young, she had little hope of going pro. She was part of a big family. Her mom worked multiple jobs but had trouble paying for rent and food—let alone football fees. But with help from friends and family, Kadeisha and her family got by. And despite how busy she was, her mom was there, playing goalie as Kadeisha ran drills after school.

Kadeisha's love of the game helped get her through the hard times. And by the time Kadeisha was a teenager, she caught the eye of the world's top coaches. At 17 years old, Kadeisha debuted for Canada, and she went pro a few years after that. Today, she's hailed as one of the best defenders the world has ever seen. She is an unshakeable force on the pitch.

DID YOU KNOW?

Kadeisha is a three-time Canadian Player of the Year! She won the award in 2015, 2017, and 2020.

No matter what time of day the match is, Kadeisha's favourite pregame meal is pancakes. Ask your grown-up to help you mix up some pancakes for your pregame meal, and try some different toppings. Ideas might include fresh fruit (Kadeisha's favourite), nut butter, a dollop of yoghurt, or maple syrup. Set up a taste test and see what makes you feel fiercest.

'FOOTBALL IS MY LIFE. I THINK IT CHANGED MY LIFE FOR THE BETTER.'
—Kadeisha Buchanan

KEROLIN NICOLI

Forward

Brazil • Born 17 November 1999

Kerolin has always loved football, but there was a time when she thought she'd never play the sport again. When she was 11 years old, she felt pain in her right leg. She later learned she had a rare disease causing an infection in her bone. Even after surgery, her doctors still weren't sure she'd be able to play contact sports like football.

But Kerolin never gave up. She started kicking the ball around with friends to get her skills and strength back. Over time, her leg healed, and she was back to playing the game she loved. Kerolin rose in the ranks in the club system in Brazil and eventually her dream came true—she went pro.

In 2022, Kerolin joined the North Carolina Courage. In her first game against NY/NJ Gotham FC, she used every minute to showcase her strength on the pitch. When Kerolin received the ball from her teammate towards the end of the game, she knew she had to take her chance. She ran down the pitch, bypassing three defenders, then *WHAM*—she kicked the ball with her right foot, slamming it into the goal.

> **'I HAVE ALWAYS DEDICATED MYSELF TO ACHIEVING GREAT SUCCESSES IN MY CAREER.'**
> **—Kerolin Nicoli**

DID YOU KNOW?

Some of the best footballers ever come from Brazil, including Pelé and Marta Vieira da Silva.

FUN FACT

At 19, Kerolin was named Breakout Female Player by the Brazilian Football Confederation.

DRILL BREAK: BEAT THE WALL

All you need is a ball and a wall, so let's go!

- Pass the ball to the wall like you're passing to a friend.
- When it comes back to you, try to stop it or kick it back with a different part of your foot each time.
- How many different parts of your foot can you use? Are you able to keep control over the ball?

- This time, **throw** the ball against a higher part of the wall.

- Try to stop the ball or pass the ball back to the wall—but this time use different parts of your body, like your chest, head, and different parts of your feet.

- How many different parts of your body can you use?

WITH FRIENDS AND FAMILY

- When you're ready, get a friend or family member to join you in the challenge.

- How many times can you pass and stop the ball using your feet as a team?

- Can you stop the ball with a different part of your foot each time?

- If you like, you can test your skills against each other: Pass the ball to each other in different ways to make it challenging for your partner to stop the ball.

- Remember to support and help each other get better!

FRANCISCA 'KIKA' NAZARETH

Midfielder

Portugal • Born 17 November 2002

Kika doesn't remember a day when a ball wasn't at her feet. She started playing football as a kid with her dad in the street. They also went to Benfica games together at Estádio da Luz, a stadium in Portugal. Kika loved cheering for her home team, and she dreamed of playing in stadiums just like they did.

Her career in football started when she was 16. Kika was known to be fearless on the pitch and had a magic touch that sent the ball flying wherever she wanted it to go. At 17, Kika joined Benfica, the team she grew up watching from the stands!

> 'DO "ONE MORE" EVEN WHEN THINGS ARE DIFFICULT. YOU ALWAYS HAVE ONE MORE IN YOU.'
> —Francisca 'Kika' Nazareth

Kika even celebrated one of the most exciting wins of her career right at Estádio da Luz. It was the Portugal Women's National Championship. Kika and her team were unstoppable and beat their opponent 3–1. When the game ended, Kika and her teammates cheered and danced around the pitch that Kika had once only dreamed of playing on.

FUN FACT

Kika's favourite song to play before a match is 'Billie Bosa Nova' by Billie Eilish.

Want to have the magic touch like Kika? Try to master the one-touch pass.

- Grab a ball and a friend and head to your favourite practise space.
- Have your friend kick the ball toward you.
- Without stopping or dribbling the ball, kick the ball back to your partner.
- Once you master passing a rolling ball while standing still, see if you can do it while you're running down the pitch!

LAUREN JAMES

Forward

England • Born 29 September 2001

Lauren grew up in a football-playing family. In a big field near their home in London, Lauren and her two older brothers scrambled after the ball as their father coached them through drills. Over time, Lauren's moves became so smooth, it looked like she was gliding down the pitch. At 16, Lauren went pro, and it seemed like her career could only go up.

But then came the injuries. It was frustrating for Lauren that her body wasn't cooperating. She was impatient—she wanted to be out on the pitch. But her new coach at the Chelsea Football Club reminded her that healing takes time.

So, Lauren focused on physical therapy. Within months, she got stronger and stronger. Finally, when her coaches gave her the green light, Lauren flew across the field like a comet. In one game for England's national team, Lauren dodged past four defenders, who, desperate to stop her, finally grabbed at her jersey. In that same game, Lauren sent the football past a mob of defenders in a stunning goal—her first for England.

Today, Lauren remains a force to be reckoned with.

DID YOU KNOW?

Lauren and her brother, Reece, both play for Chelsea Football Club in London and are the first brother-sister duo to play on England's national men's and women's football teams!

> **'NOW EVERYONE HAS A FUTURE IN FOOTBALL.'**
> —Lauren James

As a kid, one of Lauren's favourite ways to practise was by kicking a football against a wall. Here's one drill to get you started:

* Set yourself up five or six feet from a wall outside. Make sure you're far away from any windows.

* Kick the ball toward the wall with the inside of your right foot.

* When the ball comes back, pass it toward the wall with the inside of your left foot.

* Repeat and see how much stronger and more in control your shots get as your practise!

Bonus Challenge: Consider trying the same drill using the same foot each time or kicking with the top of your foot near your laces instead of the inside of your foot.

LEAH WILLIAMSON

Defender

England • Born 29 March 1997

O n the pitch, Leah Williamson has multiple roles. She's a defender, helping keep opponents from scoring, and she's also a team captain. Captains are leaders on and off the pitch, and Leah's calm demeanor makes her perfect for the job.

The ability to keep a cool head served Leah well during a big challenge in her career. When Leah was 18, she scored a crucial goal that secured England's place in the U-19 European Championship—but the referee mistakenly discounted it. To correct the oversight, Leah would have to take the penalty kick *again*—five days after the match. The pressure was on.

On the evening of the kick, Leah took to the pitch. Players on both teams formed a line behind her. The goalie was crouched down, waiting to block the shot. Leah got a running start, and *thwack*! With a powerful kick she launched the ball into the air. The goalie jumped for it, but Leah's shot was too powerful. The ball skimmed the goalie's fingers and landed in the net. GOAL! Leah let out a triumphant scream as her teammates enveloped her in a hug.

> 'I'M SOMEBODY WHO LIKES TO WATCH AND LISTEN QUITE A LOT, TRY AND USE OTHER PEOPLE'S STRENGTHS AND SEE HOW I CAN CONTRIBUTE.'
> —Leah Williamson

Here's how to take a powerful penalty kick like Leah:

* As you look at the goal, imagine where you want the ball to land. Aiming for the high corners of the net is your best bet—those spots are the hardest for the goalie to reach.

* Before you kick, take some deep breaths. Penalty kicks can be a lot of pressure, so try to get your body to relax.

* Get a running start and strike the ball with the inside of your foot. Make sure to follow through with your kick for the most power.

* Practise, practise, practise! Try aiming for different spots in the goal each time you kick. Soon, you'll be a penalty kick pro.

FUN FACT

Leah is also a children's book author. Her book, *You Have the Power*, encourages girls to follow their dreams and believe in themselves.

LIEKE MARTENS

Forward

The Netherlands • Born 16 December 1992

As a kid, Lieke knew she wanted to be a professional football player, but there weren't any teams for girls anywhere near her hometown in the Netherlands. Lieke was determined to play, though, so she joined a boys' team. At first, the boys didn't think she could keep up, but soon, she was racing down the pitch at lightning speed and making impressive goal shots. At 16, Lieke joined her first professional team.

Lieke's breakout performance came at the 2017 Women's Euro. She made two crucial assists and scored three goals, including a game-winning shot against Belgium. In that same match against Belgium, her Cruyff turn had everyone talking. In one swift move, she faked out two players, spinning the ball with her heel back toward the goal. She was named best player of the tournament. Lieke held her silver trophy up high as cameras flashed. She was beaming.

Now, when she plays in front of sold-out crowds, Lieke feels proud that women's football is getting the attention it deserves.

> 'WHEN I WAS YOUNG, I HAD MEN WHO WERE MY ROLE MODELS. I REALLY FEEL I HAVE THAT ROLE NOW AND I WANT TO SHOW GIRLS WHAT THEY CAN ACHIEVE.'
> — Lieke Martens

Lieke has a Nova Scotia duck tolling retriever named Iki.

YOUR TURN!

Want to try a Cruyff turn like Lieke? Here's how:

- First, practise your dribbling skills. Grab a football and kick it around your backyard or a favourite park. Make sure the ball never gets too far away from you so you're always in control of it.

- Next, try stopping the ball with the side of your foot or your heel as quickly as you can and dribbling back in the other direction.

- Keep practising until your moves get smoother and smoother!

Bonus Challenge: Practise with a friend or family member and have them try to steal the ball away from you.

NAOMI GIRMA

Defender

United States • Born 14 June 2000

From the time Naomi could run, she was playing football. When she was a kid, she'd dribble, pass, and score with a local group for the Ethiopian community in her California town. Naomi loved being part of such a fun, supportive team.

Naomi's passion and skills led her to going pro. An exciting moment in Naomi's career was in 2022 when her team, San Diego Wave, won their first National Women's Soccer League playoff game against the Chicago Red Stars.

The game was electrifying. Naomi's team was down in the first half, striving to get back in the game and score a goal. They zipped down the pitch, working together to take back control of the ball. Naomi's ability to predict the ball's movements on the pitch was crucial. Finally, one of her teammates made the winning goal in overtime. The stadium erupted in cheers. It was a special moment for Naomi, her team, and their passionate fans.

Today, football continues to give Naomi the chance to travel the world, chase her dreams, and, most important, have fun playing her favourite team sport.

DID YOU KNOW?

This year, Naomi's team, San Diego Wave, had the largest home-opening attendance in the history of the National Women's Soccer League. More than 30,000 fans filled the stadium!

FUN FACT

Naomi is the first player of Ethiopian descent to play in the National Women's Soccer League and for the United States Women's National Soccer team.

'ENJOY THE JOURNEY. DON'T GET TOO WRAPPED UP IN CHASING YOUR DREAM THAT YOU DON'T ENJOY THE STEPS IT TAKES TO GET THERE.'
—Naomi Girma

OLIVIA CHANCE

Midfielder

New Zealand • Born 5 October 1993

Football stole Olivia's heart when she was just five years old. As a young girl, Olivia watched her older sister and her friends play football and was determined to join the fun.

When she finally made it on the field to play, she often found herself on all-male teams, where she had to fight just for a chance at the ball. At first, it made her feel insecure. But soon she learned to use her quick feet to swiftly steal the ball away. Sometimes she even stole the ball from her own teammates to prove her skills to them! Olivia found opportunities to shine.

FUN FACT

Olivia's favourite song to listen to before a game is 'Aotearoa' by Stan Walker.

One of her favourite moments in her career happened during an international friendly match against South Korea on her home turf in New Zealand. At the very beginning of the game, Olivia had the ball. She saw an opening, and *BAM*—her left foot drove the ball into the net. The crowd jumped to their feet. The cheers of family, friends, and fans buzzed all around Olivia. She looked up at the stands and raised her arms to form a heart with her hands. She was beaming.

'CELEBRATE EVERY GOAL AND EVERY BIG TACKLE!'
—Olivia Chance

Want to eat like a world champion? Grab a grown-up and try out Olivia's go-to game day recipe. It's simple: Toast a slice of bread and top with your favourite kind of cheese, avocado, and an egg any style you like. For an extra kick (pun intended!) add some spicy chili jam.

PERNILLE HARDER

Forward and Midfielder

Denmark • Born 15 November 1992

When Pernille was 10 years old, she wrote a letter to her future self. In it, she imagined she'd be a professional footballer, one of the best in the world. Growing up in Denmark, Pernille's favourite thing to do was to play football with her friends. The whole group would head to her house after school and play in the back garden. The sky would turn black, with stars twinkling overhead, and they'd still be passing, dribbling, and scoring.

But as Pernille's skills improved, the opportunities for her to play competitively in her hometown dwindled. She had to fight for a spot on a boys' team in order to continue advancing in football. It wasn't the last time Pernille would have to stand up for herself as a female footballer. In 2017, after a stellar season that took Denmark all the way to the finals at the Women's Euro, Pernille and her team went on strike, demanding fairer pay. The strike cost them some important matches, but their success empowered other teams to ask for what they deserved.

Today, Pernille is considered one of the best female footballers in the world . . . just as she predicted.

DID YOU KNOW?

In the UK, the Football Association (FA) banned professional women's football in 1921, declaring it 'unsuitable for females.' The ban was rescinded in 1971.

Grab 10 toys or objects that you don't mind knocking over. It's time to get a strike!

KICKING

- In this activity, your objects are called 'pins'.

- Arrange your pins into a triangle. The easy way to do this is to create four rows (one pin, two pins, three pins, four pins).

- Position yourself about 10 feet or about three metres from your pins.

- Pass the ball toward the pins, trying to knock over as many as possible.

- Each time, count how many you knock down. Can you beat your score each time?

- What were you doing when you were most successful?

- When you're ready, switch which foot you kick with each time.

THROWING

- Arrange the pins in a triangle, like in the kicking drill.
- Position yourself about 10 feet (three metres) away from the pins.
- Throw the ball and see how many pins you can knock down.
- To challenge yourself, try moving farther away, or arranging the pins in different shapes.

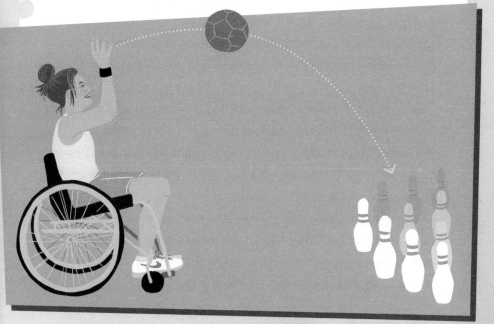

WITH FRIENDS AND FAMILY

- When you're ready, get a friend or family member to join you in the challenge.
- Create the rules so that **everyone** can play: Do you throw? Do you kick? How far away do you start from the pins?
- Be sure to always cheer on the other players, and help each other along the way!

RISA SHIMIZU

Defender

Japan • Born 15 June 1996

Risa knew she wanted to play football at just seven years old. When her older sister went to football practise, she'd tag along and kick a ball around with her dad on the sidelines. She tried mimicking the moves she saw the older girls do. Risa couldn't wait for the day she could play on a team herself.

At age 12, she was accepted into Japan's top youth football academy, which started her on her path to becoming a professional footballer. One of the biggest moments in her career was in 2021 when Risa got to compete in the biggest athletic competition in the world.

During the competition, Risa and her team were up against England in a match that would determine who would get to the knockout round. The game was challenging, but Risa fought hard. Her dark ponytail swung behind her as she raced across the pitch with boundless energy to help defend her team's goal.

In the end, England managed to get one ball past Japan and won the match 1–0. Win or lose, though, Risa is always proud of herself when she does her best. The girl who started out on the sidelines is now front and centre.

FUN FACT

As a kid, Risa was a talented runner. Thanks to that experience, she is known for her stamina on the pitch.

Defensive players like Risa are tasked with stopping the ball from getting close to their team's goal. Try your hand at defence by practising this drill. It's called 'Feed the Bears!'

- Gather a group of six friends for this game.

- Assign two people to be the bears and two people to be zookeepers. The bears and the zookeepers stand in the middle while the rest of the players form a large circle around them.

- The players in the circle try to pass the ball to the bears, and the zookeepers try to intercept it. To win a point, the players in the circle must successfully get the ball to one of the bears.

'FIND SOMETHING YOU CAN COMMIT YOURSELF TO.'
—Risa Shimizu

SAKINA KARCHAOUI

Defender

France • Born 26 January 1996

The first time Sakina's feet touched a football, she was seven years old. She was playing with kids in her neighborhood in southern France. Sakina passed and dribbled, darting this way and that. Then, she nutmegged another player—passing the ball right between his legs! Her friends whooped and shouted, impressed by her moves.

As Sakina got older, her footwork was so dazzling it was like she was dancing her way down the pitch. And after a few years of training, it was no surprise that she went pro and even played for Les Bleues, France's national team.

In 2019, she went with Les Bleues to the world championship—but she barely got to play. She hated being on the sidelines! Still, Sakina supported her team, and when the tournament was done, she trained harder than ever.

Sakina's training paid off. In 2020, she was a starting player for her club team, as they fought their way to win the UEFA Champions League. Today, Sakina's fancy footwork is taking her further than ever—to football stardom and another chance at winning the world championship.

> 'MENTAL ATTITUDE IS VERY IMPORTANT. FOOTBALL'S A GAME THAT ISN'T JUST PLAYED WITH YOUR FEET.'
> —Sakina Karchaoui

YOUR TURN!

Want to have fancy footwork like Sakina? Here's how to learn her signature move—the stepover.

⭐ **Set Up:** Put your right foot just behind and to the side of the ball (at about 5 o'clock if the ball is a clockface). Turn your body toward the left—the direction you're faking to go.

⭐ **Fake a Pass:** Bring your right foot over and around the front of the ball (the ball should now be at the side of both feet). This makes it look like you're kicking the ball—but you're not!

⭐ **Make Your Move:** Use the outside of your right foot to push the ball toward the right, and then run after it.

JI SO-YUN

Midfielder

South Korea • Born 21 February 1991

When Ji was a kid, a silly mix-up changed her life forever. The coach of her elementary school's boy's football team suggested that Ji join the team, not knowing she was a girl! Ji couldn't join the boys' team, but the coach wanted to train her anyway. He knew Ji had talent.

As she practised her dribbling, passing, and scoring, Ji became a magician on the pitch. Her ability to move the ball down the pitch at lightning speed with confidence and precision made her a must-watch player. She started her professional career in 2011.

Then in 2021, in an important tournament in Asia, Ji made history. During a match against Mongolia, the ball landed in front of Ji's left foot. She did what she does best—she kicked with confidence! With a swoosh the ball landed in the net, and Ji became Korea's all-time leading goal scorer across all teams, divisions, genders, and competitions. The historic moment was a dream come true for Ji.

FUN FACT

Ji has been named South Korea's Women's Footballer of the Year six times.

'[FOOTBALL] IS WHAT MAKES ME FEEL ALIVE.'
—Ji So-Yun

DID YOU KNOW?

In 2022, Ji was appointed co-president of the Korean Pro-Footballer's Association, becoming the first woman to ever occupy the role.

THEMBI KGATLANA

Forward

South Africa • Born 2 May 1996

When Thembi played her first match in her hometown of Mohlakeng, South Africa, she was nervous. It was unheard of for a girl to play football with the boys. As she took to the pitch that day, Thembi felt like all eyes were on her. But Thembi didn't let what other people thought stop her from playing her best. She scored goal after goal on her small town's dirt pitch, then went on to play in massive arenas with fans cheering for her.

During the Women's Africa Cup of Nations, Thembi helped secure South Africa's spot in the finals. One of her teammates kicked the ball toward the goal, but a player on the opposing team blocked it, sending it back down the field. Thembi didn't think twice—while the ball was still midair she drew her leg back and then launched it forward, striking the ball into the corner of the net. With a *whoosh*, it sailed just past the keeper's fingertips.

Thembi was named Player of the Tournament, just one of many accolades she's received in her professional football career so far. And it all happened because as a little girl she decided to be brave.

DID YOU KNOW?

Nigeria is the most successful nation to play in the Women's Africa Cup of Nations. Their team has won the tournament 11 times!

Thembi comes from a family of athletes—her dad played football and her mom was a sprinter.

'DON'T LET SOMEONE ELSE CHOOSE FOR YOU WHAT YOU WANT TO DO WITH YOUR CAREER.'
—Thembi Kgatlana

Who or what inspired you to pursue a career as a football coach?

As a kid I participated on different football teams, and I dreamed of becoming a professional player. Two different recruiters asked me to join their teams, but my family wanted me to put school first, and my parents' schedules as well as our economic situation at that time did not allow me to train with them. But when Proyecto Cantera came to the school where I was an elementary school teacher, I realized how excited I was to be able to teach the sport I love the most, especially to girls.

Do you remember your first experience with football?

I learned to play football along with my twin sister. One of our older brothers taught us because he didn't have anyone else to play with. Also, my dad and my two brothers used to play on football teams on the weekends, and my whole family and I went to the matches to cheer them on. When I started playing on formal teams my dad became my coach. He taught me how to sprint fast, to hit the ball with my head, and to position my waist correctly to make a shot.

What advice do you have for girls who want to succeed in sports?

Never doubt that the pitch is the space where you belong, and that we, as women, can stand out in any sport. Through sports, you can meet a lot of people who can become your friends and mentors. You can learn how to communicate, solve conflicts, be disciplined, work harder and go further, coexist, be a leader, and much more.

What advice do you have for girls who aren't sure what sport to try?

Try as many different sports as you can, identify the one where you feel most comfortable, and then just enjoy and let yourself flow in it.

How do you give constructive feedback?

My technique is called the Sandwich: I tell the player something positive, then an opportunity area, and finish with a different positive comment. When giving feedback, it is also important to recall other moments when their performance has been great, because even though the day may not have been the best, it is essential to keep them motivated. I finally add that if I ask something from them, it is because I know they can do it.

What changes would you like to see happen in women's football to make it a better environment for athletes and fans?

Give women players the value they deserve; they are high-performing athletes. I hope women's teams are able to play all their matches in their own stadiums, that they have equal pay, that all their games are streamed on TV, and that they're recognized as professional players.

Can you tell us about a big, exciting moment in your career?

My team was in a final, and we were losing 3–0. I was captain, and I kept encouraging the team. We gave everything and eventually won on penalties. We were champions!

What would you tell a girl who says 'I can't'?

'No' actually means 'not yet', because with training and consistency, everything is possible.

What are some self-care tips you give to young athletes?

You must prioritize your mental health. Winning a medal or being number one is not the most important thing. Enjoying your game and being a role model to other girls—that's what's important! Give yourself time, sleep well, and get your annual check-ups at your doctor's office.

What do you say to athletes when they lose a match or don't play as well as they would have liked?

The most important thing is to have fun and enjoy the sport that we love. Obviously winning feels amazing, but we also learn a lot when we lose, and we need to recognize the winning team. Maybe today we didn't make it, but we'll have more opportunities.

Coach Q&A
SARINA WIEGMAN
Manager of the England Women's National Team

Do you remember your first experience with football?

My first experience was playing with my brother. I played on a boys' team, which was illegal at that time. What I remember most at that time were the evening games, with lights on all over the stadium.

Since the moment I could walk, I wanted to play with a ball—football—but also just throwing balls and other team sports.

Who or what inspired you to pursue a career as a football coach?

When I was young, a woman was not able to be a coach, so I knew from a very young age that I wanted to be a PE teacher because that was where I could be in the environment I liked. And, over time, there were more opportunities; so, when I stopped playing football, I could become a coach—an amateur coach. I thought I would be a PE teacher and a coach on the side so I could do both. But then the game developed so much that I was able to become a professional coach.

What advice do you have for girls who want to succeed in sports?

Enjoy, first enjoy, and then follow your dreams. Don't let anyone tell you that you can't be what you want to be.

What advice do you have for girls who aren't sure what sport to try?

I think every girl and boy should just try out things that they like. And if you like football the most, you can stick with football, but if you like another sport the most, then do that because it's all about enjoying what you are doing. Playing sports is good for your social development, emotional development, and physical development. It's good for your confidence too, so just go for it.

How do you give constructive feedback?

I think we all have the same goal: We want to become the best we can be, and we need to always be honest with each other to do so. I tell athletes to always see what the strengths of the people you work with are. Develop your strengths and work on the things you are not as good at, step-by-step. It's also very important to accept mistakes.

What should a girl say if people tell them football is not for girls?

I think the environment is changing. We have proven now that football is a sport for everyone and that it should be inclusive. Whoever you are, whatever you look like, football is for you. We may still have some people who disagree, but there are so many people now who are accepting everyone in the game. We still have battles to win, but it is becoming more and more inclusive.

What changes would you like to see happen in women's football to make it a better environment for athletes and fans?

I think we have a pretty good environment. I think the uniqueness of the women's game is that it is inclusive, very inclusive, and very approachable. We are very close to the fans. Now when you go to a game, while it is very competitive, it is calm, it is relaxed, with really nice people around as fans. We should do everything we can to keep it that way.

Can you tell us about a big, exciting moment in your career?

I have a couple of big moments I am thinking about when it comes to my career as a coach—of course winning two Euros with the team I work with. Another highlight is the final at the world championship 2019. But one of the most exciting games that I have been part of was the game against Spain in the semifinal of the Euro in 2022. Everything came together in that game. That was very, very exciting. So there are just so many moments that I really enjoyed and that I cherish. They will always stick with me, but I am mostly looking forward to the next ones coming up.

What would you tell a girl who says 'I can't'?

Don't underestimate what you are capable of if you go for it. Trust yourself.

NIKE FC COMMUNITIES

Nike works with incredible communities around the world dedicated to encouraging girls everywhere to get out and play!

HIJABI BALLERS
Toronto, Canada

CENTER FOR HEALING AND JUSTICE THROUGH SPORT
Chicago, United States

GIRLS IN THE GAME
Chicago, United States

HOLLENBECK POLICE ACTIVITIES LEAGUE
Los Angeles, United States

AMERICA SCORES NEW YORK
New York City, United States

PROYECTO CANTERA
Mexico City, Mexico

FOOTBALL BEYOND BORDERS
England

GIRLS UNITED
London, England

SPORT DANS LA VILLE
Pantin, France

FUTEBOL DU FORCA
France

FAVELA STREET FOUNDATION
Amsterdam, the Netherlands

PROJECT FEARLESS
Amsterdam, the Netherlands

BUNTKICKTGUT
Germany

WE MEET UP SPORTS
Seoul, Korea

YAMATO SYLPHID
Japan

FONDAZIONE LAUREUS SPORT FOR GOOD ITALIA
Italy

GIRLS GOT GAME
Metro Manila, Philippines

CHONBURI SPORTS SCHOOL
Chonburi, Thailand

FC BARCELONA
Barcelona, Spain

SPORTSEC
KwaZulu-Natal, South Africa

FITZROY LIONS
Victoria, Australia

NIKE FC COMMUNITIES

AMERICA SCORES NEW YORK
New York City, United States

America SCORES was started in 1994 in Washington, DC, by public school teacher Julie Kennedy, who noticed that her students had limited access to after-school activities. Kennedy realized that the combination of two seemingly unrelated activities—poetry and soccer—could complement each other as both offer opportunities for self-expression, performance, and group support. Today, America SCORES has a presence in 11 cities in the United States and Canada.

BUNTKICKTGUT
Germany

Founded in 1996, Buntkickgut provides refugee children with a supportive community and a safe place to play football and make lasting friendships. In its first year, the organization had ten participating teams—now they have more than 100.

> 'Favela Street has shown me that you can achieve your goals if you put in the effort.'
> —FAVELA STREET PARTICIPANT

CENTER FOR HEALING AND JUSTICE THROUGH SPORT
Chicago, United States

Center for Healing and Justice through Sport (CHJS) is a national nonprofit organization working to ensure that more young people have access to sport experiences that are youth-centred, healing-centred, inclusive, and that work to address issues of systemic injustice. CHJS believes that nothing heals like sport.

CHONBURI SPORTS SCHOOL
Chonburi, Thailand

Chonburi Sports School was founded in 1999 to give students the opportunity to play sports without worrying about tuition fees. Chonburi Sports School is dedicated to creating equal opportunities for boys and girls in Thailand to excel in sport.

FAVELA STREET FOUNDATION
Amsterdam, the Netherlands

Favela Street Foundation was founded in 2014 in Rio de Janeiro, Brazil, with two main goals: to provide girls and boys a fun and safe environment to play football, and to train athletes to become football coaches in their communities. Today, Favela Street serves marginalized communities around the world.

FC BARCELONA
Barcelona, Spain

The Barça Foundation was launched in 1994 with the mission to improve the lives of vulnerable children and teens through sports. Participants of FC Barcelona's football programs are welcomed into a community where they learn valuable skills like teamwork and perseverance.

FITZROY LIONS
Victoria, Australia

Fitzroy Lions was formed in 2013 to give kids of all socioeconomic backgrounds a chance to play football. The foundation strives to create an environment where all participants can feel valued, supported, and respected, regardless of their background or skill level.

FONDAZIONE LAUREUS SPORT FOR GOOD ITALIA
Italy

Fondazione Laureus Sport was founded in 2001. The organisation offers free sports to girls and boys from vulnerable socioeconomic backgrounds. Fondazione Laureus Sport's mission is to inspire cohesion within communities, fight against gender stereotypes, and support the growth of at-risk boys and girls.

FOOTBALL BEYOND BORDERS
England

Football Beyond Borders (FBB) works with young people from areas of socioeconomic disadvantage who are passionate about football but disengaged at school. FBB helps students finish school with the skills and grades to make a successful transition into adulthood.

FUTEBOL DU FORCA
France

Futebol Du Forca began with one football team on a dirt pitch in Mozambique more than 10 years ago. It is now a leading global organization empowering close to 30,000 girls.

GIRLS GOT GAME
Metro Manila, Philippines

In May of 2015, a group of former university athletes led by Krizanne Ty and Nikka Arcilla founded Girls Got Game. Through free sports camps, they pass on the valuable life skills that they learned through sports to young Filipinas from underprivileged communities.

NIKE FC COMMUNITIES

GIRLS IN THE GAME
Chicago, United States

In 1995, a group of women set out to ensure that girls in Chicago had access to sports and fitness opportunities. Through Girls in the Game, they create programs that bring the joy and positivity they found in sports and movement to girls in their community.

> 'Girls in the Game allowed me to learn, grow, and lead.'
> —MARIYA, GIRLS IN THE GAME ALUM

GIRLS UNITED
London, England

Girls United was founded in 2017, with the mission to provide girls the opportunity to play football and learn valuable life skills. The organisation started with a handful of participants and has grown to include more than 130 coaches and 4,500 participants.

HIJABI BALLERS
Toronto, Canada

Amreen Kadwa founded Hijabi Ballers in 2017 when she was just 22 years old. Amreen realized there wasn't an organisation uniting and celebrating women in the Muslim community who played sports. Through Hijabi Ballers, Amreen is increasing opportunities for Muslim women and girls in sports.

HOLLENBECK POLICE ACTIVITIES LEAGUE
Los Angeles, United States

Founded in 1992, the Hollenbeck Police Activities League (HPAL) was created by Hollenbeck Police and Boyle Heights residents to implement services for high-risk youth. HPAL provides youth in their area with high-quality sports, education, and career development programs.

> 'I no longer fear the ball. I run faster, I make more goals, and feel better!'
> —ISABELLA, HPAL PARTICIPANT

PROJECT FEARLESS
Amsterdam, the Netherlands

Founded in 2019, Project Fearless is a space for girls and genderfluid youth in Amsterdam to break stereotypes, use their voice, and make an impact. From football to entrepreneurship, their one-of-a-kind programs support kids during their formative years.

PROYECTO CANTERA
Mexico City, Mexico

Proyecto Cantera was born out of a desire to support children and teens living in vulnerable situations in Mexico City. The organization uses football to promote inclusion and life skills. Today, Proyecto Cantera works with 680 participants from 17 partner institutions.

SPORT DANS LA VILLE
Pantin, France

Sport dans la Ville creates innovative educational programs dedicated to serve youth at every stage of their development. Today, Sport dans la Ville is France's leading nonprofit, serving more than 10,000 underprivileged children through sports and job-readiness training.

SPORTSEC
KwaZulu-Natal, South Africa

Sportsec originated in 2006 with the aim to customize and deliver sustainable sports programs in marginalized communities. Sportec's programs encourage young people to make better choices, avoid risks, and stay healthy on a physical, mental, and emotional level.

WE MEET UP SPORTS
Seoul, Korea

We Meet Up Sports was founded by two retired female footballers who realized there weren't many opportunities for female athletes after retirement in Korea. The organisation makes it possible for adult athletes to continue pursuing their passion by coaching girls in various sports.

YAMATO SYLPHID
Japan

Yamato Sylphid was founded by two talented footballers who couldn't find places for them to play as girls past the age of 12. They created an environment for girls and women to continue enjoying football. In 2011, a team formed at Yamato Sylphid went on to win the women's world championship!

SPORTS BRA 101

Sports bras are designed for play and movement. A good-fitting sports bra will make you feel comfortable and confident getting out onto the field, court, mat, or wherever your sport takes you! Here's how to find the perfect sports bra for you:

FIND YOUR TYPE: Most sports bras for girls fall into two categories: light support and medium support. Light support bras are usually made of a thinner, stretchy material and have skinny straps. These bras are perfect for exercises like walking, yoga, stretching, or ballet. Medium support bras are typically thicker and have wide straps. These bras fit a little tighter and support your breasts when you do high-impact activities like running and jumping.

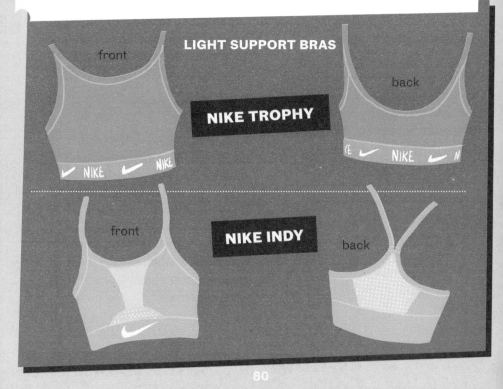

LIGHT SUPPORT BRAS

front

back

NIKE TROPHY

front

NIKE INDY

back

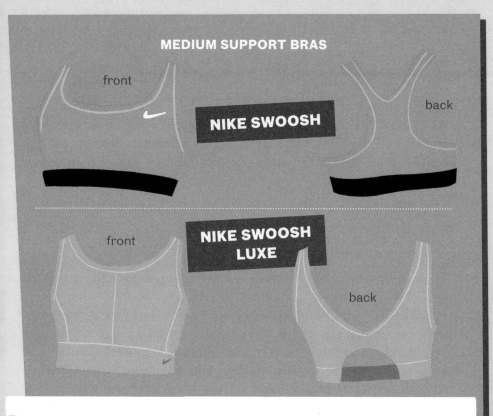

front

NIKE SWOOSH

back

front

NIKE SWOOSH LUXE

back

MEASURE: Wearing one of the bras you already have or just a T-shirt, use a soft tape measure and wrap it around the fullest part of your chest. Take note of this number—this is your band size and coordinates with the size of bra you'll want to try on. Nike uses a sizing chart that you can find online. Just find the measurement you took and match it to the size on the chart. For instance, 73–79 cm would be a size medium.

TRY IT ON: Pick a few styles and see how they feel. Make sure the straps and band around your back feel secure, but not too snug. The bra should fit smoothly under your arms without any gaping or bunching. Try stretching, running, and jumping to make sure you feel comfortable and supported moving around. Then, make your purchase and get outside and play!

Did you know that 70 percent of girls avoid being active when on their period? Many girls are worried about leaking or have trouble finding workout clothes that they feel comfortable in. But physical activity on the days when girls have their period is super important. Exercise is proven to:

- ☀ Reduce uncomfortable symptoms like cramps
- ☀ Boost energy and mood
- ☀ Provide relief from anxiety

Period-proof bottoms are a great way to stay active during that time of the month and feel confident while doing so! Check out **Nike's Leak Protection Biker Shorts**. The sleek design will move with you, and the absorbent liner acts as a secure backup to your usual form of period protection. Nike's Dri-FIT technology wicks away sweat, keeping you dry and cool, and the design includes two hidden pockets for phone or key storage. Run, dance, jump, and score without worry in these ultra-comfortable shorts.

NIKE LEAK PROTECTION BIKER SHORTS

hidden pockets

Dri-FIT fabric

absorbent liner

outer view

inner view

Every girl should have the tools and products that allow them the opportunity to play the sports they love. And for some girls, that includes a hijab. For Muslim women, the hijab is a symbol of their religion and for many, it is a part of their daily lives. But everyday hijabs aren't made for exercise. They're looser fitting and may slip or get tangled. That's where the **Nike Sport Pro Hijab** comes in.

NIKE SPORT PRO HIJAB

Here are some tips for trying it out:

Use the straps inside to prevent slippage. They tuck just behind your ears and secure the hijab in place.

Style your hair in a low bun at the base of your neck. This prevents any uncomfortable bunching and ensures a smooth, easy fit.

Try on different sizes to find the best fit for you. Run, jump, and stretch while you're testing them out to see how it will feel when you're out on the field.

On game day, tuck the hijab into the neckline or collar of your jersey so that the material doesn't get in your way. Then, play your heart out!

AUDIO ADVENTURES

LISTEN TO MORE EMPOWERING STORIES ON THE REBEL GIRLS APP!

Download the app to listen to beloved Rebel Girls stories, as well as brand-new tales of extraordinary women. Filled with the adventures and accomplishments of women from around the world and throughout history, the Rebel Girls app is designed to entertain, inspire, and build confidence in listeners everywhere.

Lea Schüller

Klara Bühl

Magdalena Eriksson

Check out these bonus audio interviews with more world champions! Scan the codes to listen. Available starting the 13th of July.

Ella Toone

Kadeisha Buchanan

SPORTS BRA 101: THE FIT CARD

Ready to find the perfect bra for your chosen sport?
Cut out the card below and you'll have some handy tips
and tricks to take with you when you go shopping.

Follow this checklist when trying on sports bras:

☐ My chest feels comfortable and supported when I move around.

☐ The straps are fitted but not too tight.

☐ The band sits comfortably around my body without digging in or feeling too loose.

☐ There's no annoying gaping or bunching under my arms.

☐ I feel confident and ready to play!

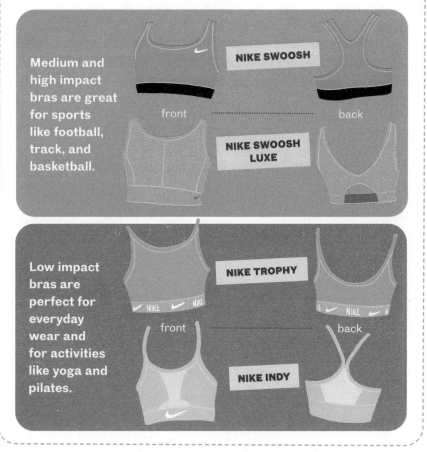

Medium and high impact bras are great for sports like football, track, and basketball.

NIKE SWOOSH

front .... back

NIKE SWOOSH LUXE

Low impact bras are perfect for everyday wear and for activities like yoga and pilates.

NIKE TROPHY

front .... back

NIKE INDY

At **NIKE**, we believe that if you have a body, you're an athlete, and that the future of sport is creative, inclusive, and limitless. We know the next generation—your generation—isn't thinking about creating in the future—you're leading the way now.

For us, change starts with listening to the voice of the athlete. So we're listening to your voice! Yes, you, the person who made their way to the end of this book!

We want to know and learn about your perspective on the world and how your relationship to sport is unlike any other generation that's come before. We want to understand more about the emotional and physical barriers that you face today—in sport and in life.

The more we listen, the more we learn. And the more excited we are about the chance to redefine sport with and for your generation.

We believe play is the gateway. We want you to remember that you don't do sports—you *play* sports and we want to inspire every athlete to get out and play!

For more stories about amazing women and girls, check out other Rebel Girls books.

REBEL GIRLS is a global, multi-platform empowerment brand dedicated to helping raise the most inspired and confident generation of girls through content, experiences, products, and community. Originating from an international best-selling children's book, Rebel Girls amplifies stories of real-life women throughout history, geography, and fields of excellence. With a growing community of nearly 23 million self-identified Rebel Girls spanning more than 100 countries, the brand engages with Generation Alpha through its book series, award-winning podcast, events, and merchandise. With the 2021 launch of the Rebel Girls app, the company has created a flagship destination for girls to explore a wondrous world filled with inspiring true stories of extraordinary women.

As a B Corp, we're part of a global community of businesses that meets high standards.

Join the Rebel Girls' community:
- Facebook: facebook.com/rebelgirls
- Instagram: @rebelgirls
- Twitter: @rebelgirlsbook
- TikTok: @rebelgirlsbook
- Web: rebelgirls.com
- App: rebelgirls.com/app

ILLUSTRATIONS:

Pg. 7: Juliette Toma. Pg. 9: Montse Galbany. Pg. 11: K. Wroten. Pg. 13: Natalia Agatte. Pg. 15: Sofia Moorefield. Pg. 16-17: Georgia Rucker. Pg. 19: Sarah Madden. Pg. 21: Sofia Cavallari. Pg. 23: Janie Secker. Pg. 25: Taina Cunion. Pg. 27: Britney Phan. Pg. 28-29: Georgia Rucker. Pg. 31: Joanne Dertili. Pg. 33: Kaitlin June Edwards. Pg. 35: Eve Archer. Pg. 37: Tatsiana Burgaud. Pg. 39: Janeen Constantino. Pg. 41: Camila Ru. Pg. 43: Camila Anselmé. Pg. 44-45: Georgia Rucker. Pg. 47: Alessandra Berenato. Pg. 49: Kim Holt. Pg. 51: Lynn Bremner. Pg. 53: Bodil Jane. Pg. 55: Salini Perera. Pg. 57: Cinthya Álvarez. Pg. 59: Rut Pedreño. Pg. 60-61: Georgia Rucker. Pg. 63: Vivian Mineker. Pg. 65: Monet Alyssa. Pg. 67: Lucy Zhang. Pg. 69: Lydia Mba. Pg. 70: Georgia Rucker. Pg. 72: Georgia Rucker. Pg. 80-83: Georgia Rucker.